A Devotional of 52 Lessons from Two Years of Running a Football Bantering Facebook Group

A Satire Devotional By **C.K. Eu**

WARNING: If you do not understand satire or irony, do not read this devotional book. You might damage your phone screens if it is an ebook. No compensation claims will be entertained for damages caused while reading this book.

This book is dedicated to:

my wife,

my daughter,

my favourite club Manchester United,

THE Facebook group I moderate,

and lastly,

all football fans worldwide.

"By all means marry. If you get a good wife, you'll be happy. If you get a bad one, you'll become a philosopher. "– Socrates

PREFACE

Although sports and football are often referred to as an industry these days, it always had been a philosophy to me. Football had been a part of my life since young. And I had been supporting my club since I was 8-9 years old. Matches were shown free on TV those days.

My neighbour and I are rivals. I am not exaggerating when I said that I had been laughing at him for about twenty years until Sir Alex Ferguson retired. Then, I moved away. (yes, this is where you break a chuckle.)

This devotional, or book, is not one that you read with a straight or stern face. You read it to get chuckles here and there. You read it to relax and not think about anything else but looking for an opportunity to smile.

My life philosophy is simple. Work hard, play hard, respect all. It is the same with my footballing philosophy and how I manage my teams (on the games Football Manager and Championship Manager since 1998).

Maybe I got a bad wife or I got "married" to a bad club, I am a lot more philosophical these days. A smile a day brightens your day and those you met after. This is a satire piece so take it in good humour. No names will be mentioned unless for a good cause.

Yours-in-Bantering.

"You can't win anything with kids." – Alan Hansen

"I learned all about life with a ball at my feet" – Ronaldinho

"Football. Bloody football." – Sir Alex Ferguson

"Some people think football is a matter of life and death. I don't like that attitude. I can assure them it is much more serious than that." – Bill Shankly

Week 1

"This is Our Year!" is great but do follow up your enthusiasm with hard work.

Every New Year Day is a happy day, so is beginning of each season. We cannot avoid getting all excited and shout.

"This is going to be our year!"

"This is my best year yet!"

"I am going to fulfil all my New Year Resolutions!"

Every new beginning is nice. It warms my heart to moderate posts of high hopes at the beginning of each season. I see fans posting how great this new signing is. I see "best of xyz" videos. I see players saying they are going to clubs to win trophies. It is nice. It pumps you up.

Sadly, most new signing (these days) doesn't living up to the hype on day one. Just ask United fans.

Enthusiasm is great. Please follow up your enthusiasm with hard work. Hard work and enthusiasm are mutually infectious.

Week 2

Settle scores early, or when you have the chance to.

I had seen, and engaged in, banter threads that span pages. There is a certain individual in the group that I like to banter with, and we could go on for quite a while. This might come across as childish, having nothing better to do, or just whiling time away.

But you feel great after that. There is a relief at the end of it. You feel satisfied after a great and long banter where it ends when it ends.

We feel great because there is a closure. I might had lost the banter. I might had won it. But it is closure. There is a definite outcome.

Please settle your scores early and not late. Do not leave over time. Do not say "I will get back on you someday." Do not harbour grudges. It only bothers and hurts you, not them.

Settle it now or when you got a chance to. Do not leave it.

Week 3

Rinse. Dry. Repeat......Act Different!

Sometimes, you get a setback early in the year. And we get that same old "rinse, dry, repeat" feeling. The same old thing happened again.

It is like the 7-up memes popping up whenever Man United plays Liverpool, or the iconic Stevie Gerrard Slip gets a mention when Liverpool falters. (As a moderator of the group, I lost count of how many times those are mentioned. I am guilty of contributing too.) Or your team started to falter barely 3 weeks in the season. Or yet another disruptive backroom news emerged.

It could be getting into debt again, losing your job or temper again.

Rinse. Dry. Repeat. What do we do then?

It is not about what we do. No one can tell you what to do about it. It is about what can I do differently.

What can I do differently to get a different result and outcome?

What can I do different to break the cycle?

Week 4

Don't blame the Referee or VAR.
Everyone has the same 90 minutes.

With the introduction of Video Assistant Referee (VAR), people have a new common enemy. It is no longer Manchester United, if anyone still remember the ABU (Anything but United) crowd. I noted a rise in posts and comments condemning VAR as well.

Don't blame the VAR or Referee.

Why could Manchester United do it in Nou Camp? Why could Liverpool keep on equalising or scoring the winning goal (to my disgust) late in the game these days?

Everyone has the same 90 minutes.

What are you making of the chances that come your way? Are you missing them like Nunez? (I can't help myself here!) Are you making your chances count?

When opportunities can come up, are you ready for it? Don't

blame the times when you are down on luck.

Blame it on the preparation you didn't commit yourself to when opportunities knocked on your door. Be prepared!

Week 5

If something spoils your fun,
stay away from it.

In life, stay happy. A happy heart and happy mind achieve more. This is the reason why I have moderators from both sides of the fence.

After the 7-0 defeat, I stayed away from the group and internet for a couple of day. I had an important meeting to attend on the Tuesday that followed. I could not allow the defeat and the banter to get into me. It spoils my mood and my fun. I stayed away.

It was tough trying to ignore all those posts tagging and messages, but I did it anyway. Barely. I kept my mind and fun and had a great meeting.

Nothing is more important in life than enjoying life itself. You enjoy life when you are having fun. So do not ever let everything takes away your fun.

Stay away from anything that spoils your fun.

Week 6

Remember that there will
always be that one guy.

In my group, there is always that one fellow who post ludicrous stuff about Liverpool. I got to confess that I love it, but I also got to say that sometimes it gotten too far. The moderators tried to take actions. I tried to. But the guy never stopped.

I learnt that if we ignore him, his posts will be pushed down. And I deleted some of the posts after a day or so. He is still a thorn today but lesser than when he first joined the group.

In life, there is always that guy who seemed to be driving everyone crazy. We can't change his behaviour, but we can change our reaction towards him.

But remember that there will be that one guy in life, regardless of the time and season. There will be.

Don't let him spoil your fun. Learn to look away when you must.

Week 7

I know we made it when I start
seeing porn being posted.

One day, I checked the group and found a couple of porn posting. I deleted them and banned the spammers. Soon, it became a daily affair to deal with it. Before I knew it, I was deleting over 10 such posts a day. It became a big distraction to the actual moderation.

I was perplexed. *Why is this happening?* I asked some other groups owner, moderators, and search on forums. It turned out that these spammers only target groups that are popular and having high engagements. I was flattered when I knew that.

We made it.

In life, we can give ourselves a little pat on the back when we started getting unwanted attention and distraction. You made it. You made a dent enough to warrant some attention.

However, please do not be distracted. Keep the enthusiasm and work hard.

Week 8

Nothing is permanent in life,
except with hard work.

When we created the group, we have 9 of us. All of us were active. Today, we have well over one thousand nine hundred members and growing. Of the 9, only 3 or 4 are still active.

Do I miss the rest of those who started the group?

Of course, I do.

But I understand that nothing is permanent in life. No circumstances you are going through, however bad, or good, is permanent in life. No one is permanent in life too.

In fact, I learnt that nothing is ever permanent, except with hard work. I admit I was not communicating enough to the rest or working hard to keep them continually engaged, so their inactivity is understood.

If we want to make something permanent in life, we got to put in the hard work to keep it. It is the same for our job, our marriage, our family and even our bantering mates.

Nothing stays without hard and conscientious effort.

Week 9

Respect priorities and you get prioritized.

When members or moderators came to me to step down from the role or group, I never say no to them. I respect that their priorities lie elsewhere. As in previous week's sharing, nothing is permanent in life.

I learnt that respecting their priorities gain me priorities elsewhere. I may have lost a good moderator, but I found another one who is willing to set the group as his priority for that period.

It is the same in life. I respect my co-workers and subordinates' need for personal time and freedom. I never micro-manage them. In return, when I needed help, they would put me on the priority list.

Respect priorities and you will get prioritized.

Week 10

Be bold and step out!

I remember the time when Liverpool won the only title in 30 odd years. The whole group exploded, at times with profanities from Liverpool fans. Don't ask me why. They seemed an angry lot. And I made them angrier.

I made a bold prediction that Liverpool will not retain the title and will finish below Man United. As expected, I was overwhelmed by the "kind words" of the Liverpool fans. But I just felt it. I was deciding if I should post it. I thought of the backlash. But I thought, be bold and step out.

The new season ended with United finishing above Liverpool. I had a fun time trolling everyone who called me names. I didn't remember who they were, but it was just fun knowing there are people watching their screen and trying to stop their hands from typing a comment.

Life is short. Life is tough. Life is too short and too tough to stay the same. The only way to not stay the same and live higher is to......

Be bold and step out!

Week 11

Step out but be ready to eat your words, if necessary.

I was flamboyant after my prediction in previous week's sharing. I became bolder, to the point of being reckless. I made other calls, but they backfired.

It was then that I realized that I have a small faithful following. I was touched. When my prediction was wrong, screenshots of my comments were posted. And I thought we only quoted famous people. I am being quoted. I had made it. (laughs)

High risk, high reward. High reward, high backlash if it goes wrong. I was made to eat my words many times. (My "following" would tell you exactly how many times but I don't recall.) Does that stop me from stepping out and be bold?

Hell, no!

I learnt another lesson. Weigh the worst consequences and decide if you can bear with it. Only step out if you are willing to bear the consequences.

Step out but be ready to eat your words, if necessary.

Week 12

Never be too quick to judge. Have some patience or some humble pie.

During a match, I will have my Facebook app open. Besides the commentary on TV, we have the twisted (and sometimes vulgar) commentary on Facebook groups. In our group, it happened regularly. There will always be someone (sometimes me) who would jump and react or judge.

"That's not a red card!"

"Ha. Ha. Ha. 2 goals down...... you will lose!"

I learnt one thing in life. Regardless of what name your belief or Faith calls the one you worshipped; they always have a great sense of humour. When you react this way, the outcome will always be exact opposite of what you thought.

That is life. Never be too quick to judge. Just because your kid did not fare well this exam, it does not mean they will flunk all future ones.

Have some patience before judging. Or you should keep your tummy empty for some humble pie.

Week 13

In all things, always maintain a bottom line that you will and could never cross.

I am not an expert in banter but I engaged in my fair share. Most would agree with me that there will always a line that we never cross.

I never joke or said negative stuff about the 96, even if the other side made derogatory remarks on Munich.

Most Liverpool fans I know would never joke or belittle Munich as well.

Something that I am proud of the group I moderated is that everywhere the opposing club is in grief, the support and respect is massive from both sides. (There are the odd clowns but they are easily drown out by the positivity.)

This is what we envision – a group bantering with respect and a bottom line. This is how we earn respect from even our enemies –

never cross the bottom line.

Week 14

My name may sound like a noodle dish,
but you probably had noodle recently.

Racism is rampant. It happens in our group too. One of my motivation to start the group is I could not find a group when I could banter more than a few days with encountering some kind of racism.

"Ching Chong Kink. Kink Tit Chng." *(my reply: 别扮可爱了！Don't act cute! You're old enough to be my father and I ain't gay.)*

"You name sound like a noodle dish." *(This is my favourite of all the racist taunt thrown at me. You almost couldn't hate it.)*

"Do they have internet in China?" *(For record, and if you are lazy to check Google Maps, Singapore is not a part of China.)*

"The English invented football. What do you Singaporeans know about football?" *(I replied that guy that we knew how not to lose an Empire to the Japanese. He went silent on me.)*

Racist taunts are pointless chatter. If you must response, just reply pointlessly. Racist thugs are simple-minded creatures. Throw them off the script, they are lost

Week 15

Do not outsource fighting for
your dignity and honour.

I used to report comments and posts for racism and hate speech, but it is pointless. 100% of the time, Facebook or other social media platform think it is fine. It is because these hate speeches and racist comments/posts are usually subtle and localized. The platforms cannot possibly know it all.

Let's take the phrase: "I see that you cannot lift up 700." I see some racism thugs showing me their gym photos or saying: "I can." That phrase if spoken in Mandarin means having copulation with his mum in my native dialect. (Note: this phrase is the banned words in my group.)

The platforms cannot possibly know it all. I cannot moderate away all racist comments. No one can.

Fight for your dignity and honour if you are offended.

Response pointlessly and never settles (racism) score late. Do it there and then. Do not harbour racism grudges. It is painful. If it bothers you, do something there and then but not kill.

Week 16

If you are bullied, response to throw them off the tracks, not off you.

Bullying is a serious issue. It is rampant on the internet. Sadly, it does happen in our group occasionally too. I kicked and banned quite a few fellows from both sides of the fence.

Bullies, like racist thugs, are simple-minded creatures. They are like a computer program. If you give an unexpected response, they could not handle it. They hanged, like a software. They are programmed to elicit a certain response from us when they push certain buttons.

The more we kept responding to them the way they expected, they will be fonder of you and never let you go.

I observed one member of the group throwing off a bully expertly. The bully were hammering him with nasty remarks. He simply responded with weather talk. After 2-3 exchanges, the bully left the group.

If you are being bullied, throw them off the tracks.

Week 17

Breathing helps to deal with anger.

The past few weeks had been about bullying and racism. That is because the EPL season would be most intense. I had learnt from moderating the group that the most intense part of the season generates more nasty comments from all sorts. Man United fans are also the angriest at that time. In my opinion, the Liverpool fans are angry all throughout the year, at least in their comments to me.

I can imagine Liverpool fans reading this week's sharing and goes, "you w*nker!"

Breathe. Breathe in. 2… 3… 4… Breathe out.

Repeat 6 times.

It is easier to get offend by remarks and comments online or even emails and messages. Breathe.

Be slow to anger. This is how I keep my fun moderating for 2 years.

Lots of breathing exercises.

Week 18

Plan for the worst: Have Big Sam's number saved in your phone.

Sam Allardyce has built an amazing reputation for being the relegation escapist. It is no surprised that whenever a team is going through a bad patch, Big Sam memes came up a lot. They are used to troll or taunt.

No matter what, all agree that Big Sam is the Plan Z when plans A to Y failed. He is the "emergency break glass" guy. In life, unexpected things happened. We can't plan for every scenario in life but we can have a backup plan for the worst case scenario.

Always plan for the worst and have a backup of backup plan. I'm not saying that you should have multiple backup plans. We should have 3 plans – Best plan, alternative plan and worst case scenario plan a.k.a Big Sam plan.

If you are a football club owner, plan for the worst and always save Big Sam's number in your phone.

Week 19

Ignore the criticism and the mob.

Regardless of the match results, there will always be angry fans.

"The best team lost!"

"Bloody VAR! That should be a goal. We want replay!"

There will always be that angry and upset individuals. Every post in the group will receive criticisms and attract angry mob. If I was given a penny each time I'm called a clown by Liverpool fans, I be vying to be the first to go to Mars with Elon Musk.

In life, there will be criticism. Each decision of yours will make someone upset, angry, or uncomfortable. That does not matter. We cannot please everyone.

Learn that we cannot, and we will not be making everyone happy.

Week 20

What goes up must come down.

Manchester United is not in a good patch these days. I dreaded the matches with Liverpool because they bring bad memories. When these derbies come along, we will have unusual number of Liverpool fans taunting and mocking Manchester United. There are times when it seemed like we are in for a good trashing. But we didn't. And we have silence for few days.

What goes up must come down.

Football, like life, revolves around a cycle. Sometimes, we are in good form when everything seems smooth sailing. Even that bounce off the butt falls perfectly for the striker to smash in a goal. Other times, even the clearance you did thousands of times in your career, ended up in your own net.

But there is always that turning point. If we focus, work and determine to do so until the breakthrough, we will have our turning point.

Then, what comes down will always go up.

Week 21

Liars see liars everywhere. Good lad sees good lad everywhere too.

I get called liars or dishonest all the time. For the record, I never lie on my posts. If I claim something, I had the proof. Once, I posted that I betted on Liverpool losing against a minnow. I got called a liar and I showed my proof. The angry became silent.

But I understood those who called me liars or names. I have this view: What we comment online reflects our inner thoughts and well-being. Lacking the context of body language and other factors, we subconsciously turned to our inner state of mind to evaluate stuff we see online.

If we have this mistrusting mindset, we will not trust anything at all. If we are always bending around the truths, we will think everyone else is doing the same.

I am guilty of this behaviour at times. Sometimes, I get carried away with racist remarks. But we must remember that as much as liars see liars everywhere....

Good blokes see good blokes everywhere too!

Week 22

We all need an avenue to release
those steam. Find yours!

This is the time of the year when we are approaching the end of the season. Emotions are high. I also notice that there is increased amount of emotionally charged comments whenever there are:

- End of seasons.
- Financial year ending.
- Bill and Loans due.
- Mid-term reviews.

Everyone sees football differently. I see football as a form of therapy. We all have stress in life, but most do not have ways to release it when we are cooked.

I see people venting through bantering. I don't mind that in my group if it is respectful. This is after all, an avenue I seek to relieve some stress as well.

We all need a place to vent. Find yours. It is important for our mental health.

Week 23

You are only responsible to those who shared your life, not everyone whom you come across.

Our group has 1.9k members and about 2k visitors each week. It is hard to fulfil and please all of them. From this, I learnt this important lesson.

I am only responsible to the members and, especially the active ones. The visitors are going to comment a couple of times when we got some hotly discussed topics like Manchester United – Liverpool derbies. Then, they disappeared.

That is a fact.

We are responsible to those who stay in our lives – our inner circles of friends, families, and relatives. Those are the ones who we should not ignore when they criticize.

Remember that you are not responsible for everyone whom you

come across, only those who shares your life.

Week 24

There is nothing to play for. Really, or not?

Towards the end of the season, the table is shaping up. The relegated teams are clear by now. And it is also clear Tottenham would miss out on trophies again. I always note that the members are silent if our teams are not in the running for anything. There is nothing to play for.

This is also the time we see upsets like a relegated team suddenly playing like Real Madrid and beat the champion. Is there really nothing to play for the relegated teams?

There is something to play for. The relegated team may have nothing to play for, but their players have! Their players could still play in the Premier League the following season if they play well and got bought by other clubs.

The motivation comes from your why (your purpose in life), not your circumstances. In life, we may find ourselves in circumstances that we feel that there is nothing to play for.

Do not be discouraged. Revisit your purpose, embrace it and fight for it. This is what you are playing for.

Week 25

To play every game like a final,
you got to be in the final.

Both Zinedine Zidane and Pep Guardiola said it to their teams – every game is a final. Once I comment this about United in the group. Unsurprisingly, there were a lot of engagements. One comment stuck out and I got nothing to reply with, except waving a white flag.

"Win your semi-finals first." That was when United was kicked out of the Europa Semi-final. That was a good banter.

To play every game like a final, you got to be in the final. We must qualify to be there, beat the opponents with that one chance in the knockout competition.

In life, it is the same. If we want that opportunity in life, we got to qualify for it and earn it. Nothing comes for free. It all comes with hard work. If you want that big deal, qualify for it by studying all about the client and history. If you want to live in that house, qualify for it by making enough to afford it and then maintain it. To play every game like a final, you got to be in the final.

Week 26

The middle stretch is the hardest and longest. Repetition is boring but fruitful.

Some days, I am faced with 200+ comments to review and approve. This is to phase out those scam and spams. (Yes, this is why we are relatively scam and spam free.) I would be enthusiastic in the beginning but got lethargic after 10-20 comments. This would persist for a great deal until I got to the last 1-20 comments. My enthusiasm picks up again.

It is always easy to motivate ourselves when it is the beginning or the end. The middle stretch is the hardest and longest. It is when things get tougher. It is when our initial enthusiasm runs off. It is when the effect of the morning coffee wears off.

I used to run 16km thrice a week in my younger days when I have more time, unmarried and without kids. Like moderating, the middle 10km is the hardest.

It is when I have to dig deep into my purpose and goal to put my feet one in front of the other repeatedly.

I repeated it until I reach the end of my run. Repetition may be boring but repeating the right things brings fruits.

Week 27

It is the boring 1-0 wins that win the league.

Liverpool fans always remind me of the 7-0 trashing and gloated about it endlessly. But they fell silent when I reminded them that we finished above them. We qualified for Champions league, but they barely made it for Europa league in that season.

All of us love the ups. We love the big wins, but big wins do not get us to our goals. It is the boring 1-0 wins that win the league. It is the consistent grinding of results that win the league.

In life, we look for that big break, big deals, big raise, promotion, or that special someone. But these are not the ones that brings us to our goals in life.

It is the boring daily small deals that made up the big deals. It is the inconsequential small raises that make up your big raise 5 years into the company. It is the boring consistency in reporting that earns you your promotion.

It is the consistency that counts. The 1-0 wins.

Week 28

Consistency wins you league,
but dream wins you cup.

I love cups and knockout competitions. All our group members are fun to banter with during cups and knockout competitions. For the league matches, a significant portion of our members would be reserved and refrain from big comments for fear of backlash. Not for cups and knockouts. It is like they are being released and freely engage.

Everyone dreams of going to Wembley to play in the FA Cup. Everyone dreams of a giant killing act. We all need to dream.

I know this sound contradictory from my previous weeks of sharing. It is not. It is about being practical and at the same time, dreamy.

Consistency wins you the league, but dreams win you cups.

The league is our purpose and goal. It can be a successful career in medical, or law, or football. You got to put in consistent hard work for it.

Your cups could be your dream job, dream vacation, or dream car. Dream about it and fight for it!

Week 29

You don't have to win all the time,
especially when it is inconsequential.

One of the enjoyable things about bantering with Liverpool fans is they love to win and have the last word. Sometimes, I mess with the nasty and rude ones by waiting for 1-2days before replying. He thought he had me and gloating over it. But I came back yet again. I noticed that his tone gets really irritated and frustrated. (Laughs.)

We don't have to win all the time. Do I have to win every banter? No, absolutely no. I would gladly lose if someone out bantered me. Bantering, to me, is inconsequential. It does not change your life or my life if anyone of us win the banter.

So, learn to let go of the inconsequential fights. Pick your battles and fight. Make better use of your time. We don't have to win all the time, especially when it is inconsequential.

Week 30

Being inclusive comes with a price, an obligation, and an understanding.

Some visitors to our group think it is a mess. Some think everyone just like to curse and swear. Some think the Admin and Moderators does nothing. Some asked why do I make it free and public for all to see and join in to comment?

When we started the group, we envisioned it to be an inclusive and open place for respectful banter. A place where one can banter without any afraid of being discriminated or bullied. For that to happen, we need to pay a price. The price is to live with the good, the bad and ugly, when you want to be inclusive.

We also have an obligation, as a community, to stick to our principles of respectful bantering and stick to it, even when others don't. We also need to understand that when something bad is said, it is not directed personally at us. This is how we can each help to make the world a better place – being less offendable.

Being inclusive comes with a price, an obligation, and an understanding.

Week 31

Everyone has their own idea about what's good for you, but it is only your own idea that matters.

In our group, club owners are a much-discussed topic. It can get very heated and passionate. The saga of the Glazers selling Man United lasted more than a year, with fans being vocal about what they want. Everyone was split between the eventual new owner, Sir Jim, and his competitor Sheikh Jassim.

Everyone has their own idea about who is the best owner for the club. But it may not necessary be what is good for the club. And it is not what the Glazers thought is good for the world.

In life, everyone would offer some good-will advice to us at some point in time. It is based on what they think is good for you. But we do not have to heed all of them.

We must follow our own dreams and pursue the only idea that matters – ours. At the end of the day, what's good for others might not be good for us.

Week 32

Always leave room for changes
and unexpected events

I love it when people are overconfident and started posting before the game is over. It is because half the time, they be eating humble pie. It makes my job moderating easier because there isn't much to do if the replies and comments are all "LOL".

We always meet such people in real life as well. They react so quickly that they almost always never leave room for the unexpected events. They are caught out by these unexpected events. We are all guilty of that.

Leave some room for changes in life, especially when the unexpected happen. In a football game, we can make substitutions and changes in a game.

Playing badly in the first half and being down by 2 goals, is not a death sentence. There is always room for changes and the unexpected to happen.

Week 33

Prepare all that you can. When you are out there, just give it your all.

Modern football is draining to me. There are people in the group that could list down all sort of statistics – throw ins near to penalty box, attempted left foot shot on right side of goal, etc. There is a lot of data these days. I think it takes the joy out of the game sometimes.

We will watch games and have all the stats stacked up. For example, you can have 30 over shots at goal in a game. That should guarantee goals.

No! If the opponent play and give it their all, nothing is ever going to go in. Data and statistics are good, but it means nothing in the face of a big heart.

All the data and statistics in our life (i.e. our history of failures or successes) means nothing if we wake up every morning ready to give it our all.

The next time you are facing an uphill battle, remember that heart triumph all stats. Remember 1999 Nou Camp UCL final or the 2005 Istanbul UCL final. Just give it your all.

Week 34

Consistency is not performing well every week. Consistency is doing the simple thing right every time.

"How can a player paid millions of pounds, make that kind of schoolboy error?"

"Why is he playing so badly today? What happened to last week's performance?"

I often see comments and posts blasting players for their inconsistency. For a while, I was gloating over Liverpool's inconsistent performance until United caught the same virus.

My observations are that if a team cannot do the simple thing right every time, you cannot expect them to be performing consistently. Look at Pep's Man City or Sir Alex's United. They executed the simple passes perfectly all the time. They executed the set pieces well.

To get ahead in life, it is important to be doing the simple thing right all the time. To save money consistently, we got to be paying our bills on time so we avoid the unnecessary late charges. Get the simple thing right first.

Week 35

Early bird does catch the worm, but the
patient birds get the fat worms.

We live in an instant world. When we want something, we google for the answer immediately. Typing text is too slow to get an answer so we use speech recognition. When I am hungry at night, I grab an instant noodle. When the team keeps on losing, the manager buys players. When results are bad, the manager got sacked.

We want that instant gratification. We want that instant 100+ likes, shares, and comments. We want that instant agreement that social media provide. We want our posts to go viral.

For over a year, we were at 50 members. We were not attracting attention. I would be saying my prayers if we got 20 comments in a post. But we did not waiver. We kept on bantering. We kept our patience.

Liverpool kept their patience with Klopp and they finally got the first title in 30 years. United kept their patience with SAF and they got 13 titles with him.

Patience is not a virtue. Patience is life. Early bird does catch the worm but the patient birds get the fat worms.

Week 36

Quell the passive aggressors by
being friendly with them.

We all come across passive aggressive people. These are the ones who are the most difficult to deal with whether in personal or professional life. They fall in the "not friendly, but also not unfriendly" category.

I had lots of encounters with such people in the group. There are always peeking at you from somewhere, waiting for that moment to pounce on a mistake **indirectly**.

When it comes to dealing with passive aggressive people, I learnt one simply way. Quell the aggression by being friendly with them. And you could not be too friendly with them.

Passive aggressive people are always looking for that trigger to act out their pre-mediated thoughts or aggression. Do not give them that chance. Be friendly to them. Be nice to them.

I had never seen a passive aggressive person turning aggressive to someone friendly to them. If they could not take it, they would simply run away.

Week 37

Passive aggressiveness is an attitude directed at issues, not individuals.

Most people thought that passive aggressiveness is directed at individuals. I would beg to differ. Being the group owner, Admin and Moderator allows me to read all the comments made by everyone. (If I am to continue keeping the group open, I need to know what everyone is posting and commenting.) From my study of the comments, I realized that the passive aggressive people can have a really nice side to them.

I concluded that passive aggressiveness is an attitude people held towards issues and things. For example, most, if not all, of the Liverpool fans are passive aggressive to me. They have this attitude towards me because of what I wrote about their team. And it's fair enough for them to do that.

If it is an attitude, then it had got nothing to do with you. You do not have to reflect on your wrongs or behaviour when you noticed someone is being passive aggressive to you. It got nothing to do with you.

It is simply their attitude towards their perception of you. The thing to do is to shape that perception into an actual you.

Week 38

Don't write your own book of excuses.
Let others write it for you.

If I need amusement, I will always tune in to post match interviews. To me, it is comical. Modern football is so commercialized that teams and managers got to attend post-match interviews and be asked awkward questions.

Some managers (and I shall not name the German) just shoot excuses off his mouth sometimes. I do not blame him as he is obligated to attend. But we simply do not have to find excuses all the time.

In fact, it is better for others to find it for you. There are pundits and analysts paid to do that. Let them do it.

We do not have to come out with excuses for everything that we do or not do. Sometimes, it is enough to just say a simple "sorry" for something we neglected. It is adequate to simply say "thanks and I appreciate you noticing it" for someone praising you. Do write your own book of excuses.

Let others write it for you. All we need to do is to put in our best and let the results speak for itself.

Week 39

The long list of injuries is not the problem.
The problem is we are not set for it.

Every season, we have teams have injury list longer than a toilet roll. We do have very lively discussions around this topic. I love it when people use that excuse to counter my bantering.

This is modern football, not 1930s football. Every club has its team of specialists. If we are going to play a high pressing, hard running style, then we got to setup the team and club for it. We got to have the proper fitness coaches in place. We got to have the proper physiotherapists in place. We got have the proper machines. We got to have the proper coaches who could plan properly.

An injury crisis is always expected in a football season. The question is not if we will have it but are we set up for it? Are we set up for the style of play throughout the season? Are we set up for the injury crisis?

In life, health is important. Is your healthcare in place? Is your health in place? Without a proper healthy body, we can never enjoy life to the fullest. **Don't be the guy who watches others ride roller-coaster but be the one who rides it.**

Week 40

Vent your frustrations, not your anger.

As the football season or the year heats up in the summer, there will be frustrations and sometimes, anger. Everyone will have a bad day. Everyone will have that day (or days) that your lid simply got blown off.

I had mentioned that I hope for the group to be a place for people vent their frustrations positively. I imagined it to be a place for positive relax of frustration through bantering. But we all have bad days.

That is why we accept the occasional anger comments. But we would step in and intervene once it goes into a pattern. I had banned members who ignore warnings and repeatedly vented their anger on other members with personal insults. It is uncalled for.

No one owes you or me a living. No one in your life or your group has to put up with being constantly vented at. Not even our spouses or children. If we do not want to lose our love ones, we must always remember:

Vent our frustrations, not our anger.

Week 41

Talk through our anger.
Rationalize it. "idiot-ize it."

When I first started bantering, I was wild. I made all sorts of comments and remarks. Emotions kicked in and I got fired up. After some time, I realize that I am getting angrier. So I learnt the previous week's lesson. One lesson led to another.

I began to learn to talk through my anger or emotions, not to fan it but to rationalize it. In my own words or way, it is to "idiotize" it.

I learnt to question my reactions to things. I learnt to ask two questions:

1. How much of an idiot does it make me?
2. Will I like and tolerate that idiotic version of me?

If I like and could tolerate that idiotic version of me, then I would continue the path of emotions. Otherwise, I would force myself to cut it off or simply back off and move away.

When we are anger, talk through it. Rationalize it and “idiotize” it.

Week 42

You can't win anything with
kids, or can you?

Towards the end of the season, managers would play their youth players when the table standing is clear. They could not do much damage anyway.

After the opening day 1-3 United defeat to Aston Villa, Alan Hansen said, "you can't win anything with kids." Sir Alex had just sold players like Kanchelski, Mark Hughes and Paul Ince. He brooded in youngster like Paul Scholes, Nicky Butt, David Beckham, and the Neville brothers. Giggs was already a regular although he is young. We remember them as the Class of 92.

Never underestimate the young and the inexperienced. Sometimes, youth and inexperience are the best assets to have. Sometimes, we can be too ingrained into the market to appreciate the changes that are happening and missed it. The inexperienced don't have that problem. The young lack the fear that is holding us back sometimes.

I'm not asking you to go back to act youthful or inexperienced. **I'm asking you to break free from the inhibitions or assumptions we build around ourselves. Be adventurous!**

Week 43

It is what we do in the training that matters, not the choices on the field.

Every year, there will always be a mention of child prodigy that went wrong. Everyone will remember Ravel Morrison, Paul Pogba, Pongelle Sinama, Jesse Lingard, and many others. And we always find them being mentioned in jest in our group.

It is true that not everyone can be Messi or CR7. It is also true that you don't have to walk the path of Morrison and others.

We always say that there are always two choices ahead of us, to shoot or to pass. Either of these choices have an equal chance of ending up in a miss or a goal.

It is not about the choices we make. It is about what we do in the training field that matters. For every talent that is wasted through partying, I could find great talents who party and make it big like Neymar, Ronaldinho. You could pin it to their immense talent. But you can be sure that you do not hear of them slacking in the training or not doing enough.

It is never really about the choices we make on the field. It is always about what we do off the field in training.

Week 44

Delete your failings and start over again.

Bantering can be a serious business to some. We get a lot of comments and chatter. Sometimes, comments get deleted not by the moderators. They get deleted by the commenter themselves. They may have got frustrated or even run out of things to say.

It is common to see comments deleted when someone lost the banter. We allow that and I don't give much stick about it. In fact, I think there is a lesson there.

Delete your failings and start over again. Life is not perfect nor smooth sailing. We fail. What are we doing about our failures?

Do we sit on it and dwell on it?

Do we delete it and move on?

I believe deleting it helps us to move on. When you got nothing to dwell on, you move on.

Delete your failings and start over again. Start fresh. Start anew.

Start with new energy.

Week 45

Find one thing in life and do it so
well that you are world class.

When I was younger, games like Starcraft and DOTA are very popular. Everyone plays them. Some are really good at them. In fact, some became so good at e-gaming that they made a living out of it.

I remember that when Beckham bursts onto the scene, many criticize him for lack of pace. But he was world class in crossing and freekicks. He was so good at it that his passes travelled faster than any winger could get to the byline.

Juninho Pernambucano is another player who is great at that one thing. He had scored at least 75 goals from free-kicks in his career.

We spent a significant amount of time at work. Please do not waste it at doing something you are not good at. Spend it on that one or a few things you do so well that you can become world class.

Find that one thing in life.

Week 46

Supporting a club is not about blind obedience but about exhibiting passion.

I am a member of several football-related groups. Sometimes, we lose and people started lamenting. There will always be someone who comes in and says, "trust the manager."

And I see it in the group that some fans are just blindly trusting supporting. They can say no bad stuff about the club. I love United but I also diss out on them at times. Sometimes, United is just ridiculous.

Supporting a club is about show your passion for it, not blindly following. It is the same when we raise kids or interact with our parents. We show our excitement for them and our love for them. Never should we blindly support them in all that they do. This applies to our spouses as well.

Not pointing out the err to our kids, family, spouse and parents, is guiding them to a path of destruction.

Exhibit passion and not blind obedience.

Week 47

> There are only two constants in life:
> change and the club you support.

I always love Roy Keane. When asked by his wife why he tattooed the kids' name but not hers on his arm, he answered, "they are forever my kids, but you may not be my wife forever."

As a football fan, the club we support is sacred. When you are very young, you are asked to pick a club. And it stays with you for life. I supported United since I was 9. I had paid my homage to Old Trafford and attend games. I had glued my eyes to TV, flown to Bangkok and Indonesia to meet them.

This is the club I support and it will never change. Changing it would not be disrespectful to the footballing gods. So I could brave myself to engage in bantering even after a loss.

Changes happen in life, for good or bad. There will always be changes. Do not fear them.

Lean on the club you support. Lean on the goals and dreams you have in your life when you need to. They are never changing.

Change and your pillar of love works side by side.

Week 48

Learn to draw your energy from the hate.

When I am moderating the group, I get more hate than love from people. At times, I felt like I am the only guy standing while being ripped apart by hordes of Liverpool fans. My fellow United fans appeared only when we are winning. But we do have some stubborn United fans who are ever shining.

It is easy to be motivated when things are going well and when people like you for what you are doing. It is arduous when things are not going well and when you are pushing through something unpopular. Yet, this is when character is formed.

After Liverpool won the title in 2020, I said they would not win again. That was received poorly by you know who, especially after their strong start to the following season. I persisted and kept on.

I made myself unmovable and untouchable by the nasty remarks. The louder the hate is, the louder I was. In life, it is the same. Raise above the hate.

Be resilient. Be untouchable and unmovable. Block out the hate by deleting them. In time, you will overcome.

Week 49

It is time to dream but be realistic!

Whenever a transfer window opens or about to open, we are flooded with transfer news and phtoshopped images of players in United or Liverpool. And there's always an exclusive and breaking transfer news every few hours.

Before Bellingham moved to Real Madrid, I used to see news of him agreeing to a move to Liverpool. And we got several images of him in Liverpool jersey in our group. The fact is he was in talks with a few clubs, including Real and Liverpool. It is a no brainer which club he will choose.

United is always linked to top players but I had never for once, believe that Kylian Mbappe would come to United although much is spoken about it.

It is time to dream during the transfer windows but be realistic. Be realistic about what you dream about. Be realistic because you have to manage your own expectations, so you don't fall too far down if reality doesn't measure up.

Dream but protect yourself from the failings.

Week 50

Even Santa Claus stops giving after
his bag ran out of presents.

There is something I do not understand about Erik Ten Hag's United. They all aspire to be Santa Clauses. Every Christmas, they be giving away goals, points and leads. Okay, they are doing it quite regularly and not only at Christmas.

Even Santa stops giving presents after his bag ran out of it. This United just don't stop giving. They need to take stock of themselves.

In life, we got to take stock and review ourselves regularly. Are we giving away goals too cheaply? Are we always losing possession? Are we always losing our temper? Are we always late for gatherings and events? Are we always paying late fees or cancellation fees?

We got to review and take stock to know what to give and what not to. If we don't we would run into bigger problems. When that happens, that Santa in us would ran out of presents.

So stop bloody giving points and goals away (United).

Week 51

Don't look back in anger, at least not today.

It is an irony that one of my favourite groups is the Oasis. Liam is a hardcore city fan. My favourite Oasis song is, as you guessed it, Don't Look Back in Anger.

As we close the year, it is time to end this chapter and start on a clean slate. In our first New Year, we let the bad vibes carried over to the new year. That was a mistake and I determined to make it right and delete off offensive comments before the new year, as much as I could. The clean slate helps to create a friendlier environment.

In life, there are many things that we hold on that aren't going to give us the perfect start to the year or a perfect beginning. Let it go.

Don't look back in anger, at least not today.

Week 52

All good things must come to an end, for better things to begin.

As we approach the end of the year, we are always in reflective mood. Moderating the group for these 2 years taught me a vital lesson: **all good things must come to end, for better things to begin.**

I enjoyed the early days of the group. It was good but it had to end. It had to end because we are having more well-rounded, inclusive and bantering fun from all over the world.

Arsenal's good run had to end before they went on the invincible run. I remembered that they were on a pretty good and decent run. It ended. But what begins after that, still could not be replicated today – the Invincible season.

As we conclude the year, know that all good years must end, for better years to begin.

Happy New Year!

EPILOGUE

In the Apple TV series "Ted Lasso", the striker Dani Rajas said, "football is life." It is indeed life. In football, you could learn everything about life like Ronaldinho said. (But learn the good stuff only.) The late Bill Shankly remarked that football is more serious than life and death.

Think about it.

For fans like you and me, how much of our time is spent talking, thinking, playing or watching football. If you put it down on paper and numbers, it is going to alarm you.

Football is life.

And like life, football has those moments that make you go "Football. Bloody football."

It is for those moments we live.

It is those moments we savoured.

- ☐ *1994 USA World Cup Final – Brazil vs Italy*

- ☐ *1999 Champions League Final at Nou Camp –Bayern Munich vs Manchester United*
- ☐ *2002 Korea World Cup Final – Brazil vs Germany*
- ☐ *2005 Champions League Final at Istanbul – AC Milan vs Liverpool*
- ☐ *2022 Qatar World Cup Final – Argentina vs France*

Lastly, we can win with kids.

I hope you have enjoyed your year and this satire devotional. In case you are wondering which fabulous group I was running; the details are below.

Follow the Link: https://www.facebook.com/groups/604887334015045/

Or Scan:

Credits:

Cover Image		Image by Michal Jarmoluk from Pixabay.
All Dividers		Image by Gordon Johnson from Pixabay.

Printed in Great Britain
by Amazon